SPACE EXPLORERS

Illustrations
and
Graphic project

GIULIA DE AMICIS

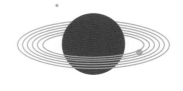
WHITE STAR KIDS

CONTENTS

WELCOME *!*

ARE YOU READY
TO *LEAVE* FOR AN

INTERSTELLAR TRAVEL

THAT WILL LEAD YOU TO
EXPLORE
THE MOST REMOTE PLACES
IN **SPACE**

?

These pages are the perfect launch pad! They have been specifically designed to satisfy the curious minds of young, brave explorers, who will have the privilege of investigating some of the most amazing phenomena in the universe.

BEFORE YOU LEAVE, HOWEVER, THERE'S SOMETHING YOU MUST KNOW: THIS IS NOT A USUAL BOOK!

Among its pages you won't find, indeed, long and complex descriptions, soaked with difficult words. Every information, every scientific fact, will be within your reach at a glance!

The text, even when dealing and explaining the most complex mysteries of the space, has been summarized in a few words and is supported by charts and colorful illustrations, which make it interesting and easy to understand.

And what about the numbers? Every astronaut knows that the numbers needed to indicate distances and orders of magnitude of the universe are really huge! However, here you'll find the numbers transformed into lines, dots and drawings that make them particularly easy to interpret.

THIS LANGUAGE, THIS PECULIAR TECHNIQUE OF COMMUNICATION THAT PUT TOGETHER GRAPHICS AND INFORMATION HAS A NAME: INFOGRAPHICS.

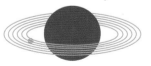

Making it easy to interpret data does not reduce, however, the fascination of a travel that begins remembering the fundamental moments of the space exploration.

You will then be able to explore in detail the Solar System, discovering what differentiates our planet from the others and what, on the other hand, makes it unique!

Past the Kuiper belt, the mysterious region that marks the border of the Solar System, there comes the time for exploring our Galaxy, the Milky Way, only to discover that it too isn't but a tiny part of the universe!

During your travel you'll meet stars thousand times bigger than our Sun, huge black holes, comets, asteroids and meteors!

In the end, you'll be able to get into a space station to understand how a human being can survive in space: those are fundamental pieces of information for a future astronaut!

ARE YOU READY TO GO?
MAKE YOURSELF COMFORTABLE,
THE COUNTDOWN HAS BEGUN!

10... 9... 8... 7... 6...

SPACE EXPLORATIONS TIMELINE

HISTORY OF MISSIONS

From the first astronomers who investigated the sky above us to the most recent progresses that allow astronauts to sail the outer space and build space stations, our space history is an incredible, exciting adventure.

1942
The German V2 rocket is the first vehicle to enter the outer space, reaching 62 miles from the Earth's surface.

1946
First pictures of Earth from space is taken from a suborbital altitude of 65 miles.

1969
American astronauts Neil Armstrong and Buzz Aldrin reach the Moon on spaceship Apollo 11 and complete the first lunar landing.

1966
First impact into another planet, Venus, with the Russian space probe Venera 3.

1961
Russian cosmonaut Yuri Gagarin is the first man in space. Gagarin's spacecraft, Vostok I, completed one orbit of the Earth in about two hours.

1971
Built by the Soviet Union, Salyut I is the first space station launched in space.

1973
Launched by NASA, Pioneer 10 is the first spacecraft to travel through the Asteroid belt. It will fly-by Neptune in 1983.

1974
The space probe NASA's Mariner 10 send to Earth the first photographs of planet Venus from space.

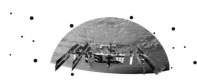

1998
The International Space Station is launched. It is the largest home for astronauts built in space.

1997
Sojourner is the first operational rover sent on Mars by NASA.

2004
NASA's Cassini is the first probe to enter Saturn's orbit and its mission is ongoing as of 2017. It will study the planet and its many natural satellites.

2005
Huygens probe lands on the surface of Saturn's biggest moon, Titan. It is the first landing on a moon in the outer Solar System.

1947
Fruit flies are the first animals in space. Used to study the effects of space journeys on living organisms, they traveled with a supply of corn to eat on the flight.

1957
The first satellite, Sputnik I, is sent in orbit by the Soviet Union and returns to Earth the first signals from space.

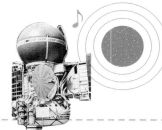

1960
Dogs Belka e Strelka spend one day in space. Along with them traveled a gray bunny, 42 mice, 2 rats, flies and a number of plants and mushrooms. They were the first terrestrial creature to orbit the Earth and come back alive.

1959
First impact into another world: the Russian space probe Luna 2 crash-lands into Earth's Moon.

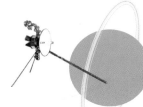

1976
Viking I is the first spacecraft to land successfully on Mars. It sent back to Earth the first photographs of Mars surface and collected soil samples.

1982
Soviet probe Venera 13 collects soil samples from Venus and records the first sounds of another world.

1990
Space probe Ulysses is sent in orbit. It will complete the first polar orbit around the Sun in 1995.

1986
Spacecraft Voyager 2 launched in 1977 flies closely past Uranus, the seventh planet from the Sun.

2011
NASA's MESSENGER spacecraft successfully achieved orbit around planet Mercury.

2015
Lettuce is the first vegetable to be grown, harvested and eaten by astronauts in space.

2016
Astronaut Scott Kelly and cosmonaut Mikhail Kornienko complete their 340 days space mission, the longest recorded time in space by NASA.

WHAT IS OUR UNIVERSE?

The universe is all of time and space and its contents. It includes planets, moons, stars, galaxies, all matter and energy. The universe is at least 13.7 billion years old and will continue to expand forever.

THE SMELL OF SPACE

Some astronauts have described the smell lingering on their space suits after a spacewalk as an acrid aroma. Others say it reminds them of seared steak. After a mission in 2003, astronaut Don Pettit tried to detail with words the smell of space. He described it as "a rather pleasant sweet metallic sensation" and "a pleasant sweet smelling welding fumes".

THE BIG BANG

The Big Bang theory is the prevailing cosmological model. It describes the development of the universe from the beginning of time and its consequent expansion.

The Big Bang can be imagined as a big, powerful explosion that happened in space about 13 billion years ago and that gave birth to all the planets, galaxies and stars of the cosmos.

3. SUPERHOT FOG

2. HOT SOUP

1. SUPERFAST INFLATION

SONGS OF THE UNIVERSE

Theoretically sound doesn't exist in space because there's no air for sound's waves to move through. But with the help of special instruments, astronomers can record the electronic vibrations of planets, moons and rings and translate them into sounds.

Every planet, moon, ring, black hole and sun emits a different sound. Finding yourself in space with a special hearing you could hear groans, metallic squeaks, hums, water's ripples, wind-like sounds and other strange, chilling noises. Those are the songs of the universe.

5. PLANETS AND STARS ARE BORN

SHAPE OF THE UNIVERSE

Astronomers don't know for certain what is the ultimate shape of the universe. They have given three possible explanation of its geometry. These possible shapes are called respectively the flat, open and closed universes.

4. GIANT CLOUDS FORM INTO GALAXIES

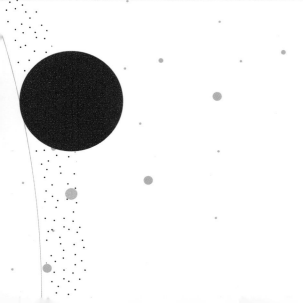

FLAT UNIVERSE

OPEN UNIVERSE

CLOSED UNIVERSE

OUR SOLAR SYSTEM

Our Solar System is part of the Milky Way Galaxy and it has formed about 4.6 billion years ago. It consists of the Sun — our star — and everything that orbits around it.

This includes the eight planets and their moons, the dwarf planets and their satellites as well as asteroids, comets and countless particles of smaller debris.

ORBITS AND STRUCTURE

We can think of the Solar System as made of two parts: Mercury, Venus, Earth and Mars compose the inner Solar System. These planets are closest to the Sun and are called the terrestrial planets because of their solid, rocky surfaces. The second part is called the outer Solar System: it includes the gas giants Jupiter, Saturn, Uranus and Neptune. Out past Neptune orbits the small planet of Pluto, which has a solid icy surface.

1 THE SUN

2 MERCURY

3 VENUS

4 EARTH

5 MARS

6 JUPITER

7 SATURN

8 URANUS

9 NEPTUNE

10 PLUTO

INNER PLANETS

ASTEROID BELT

OUTER PLANETS

KUIPER BELT

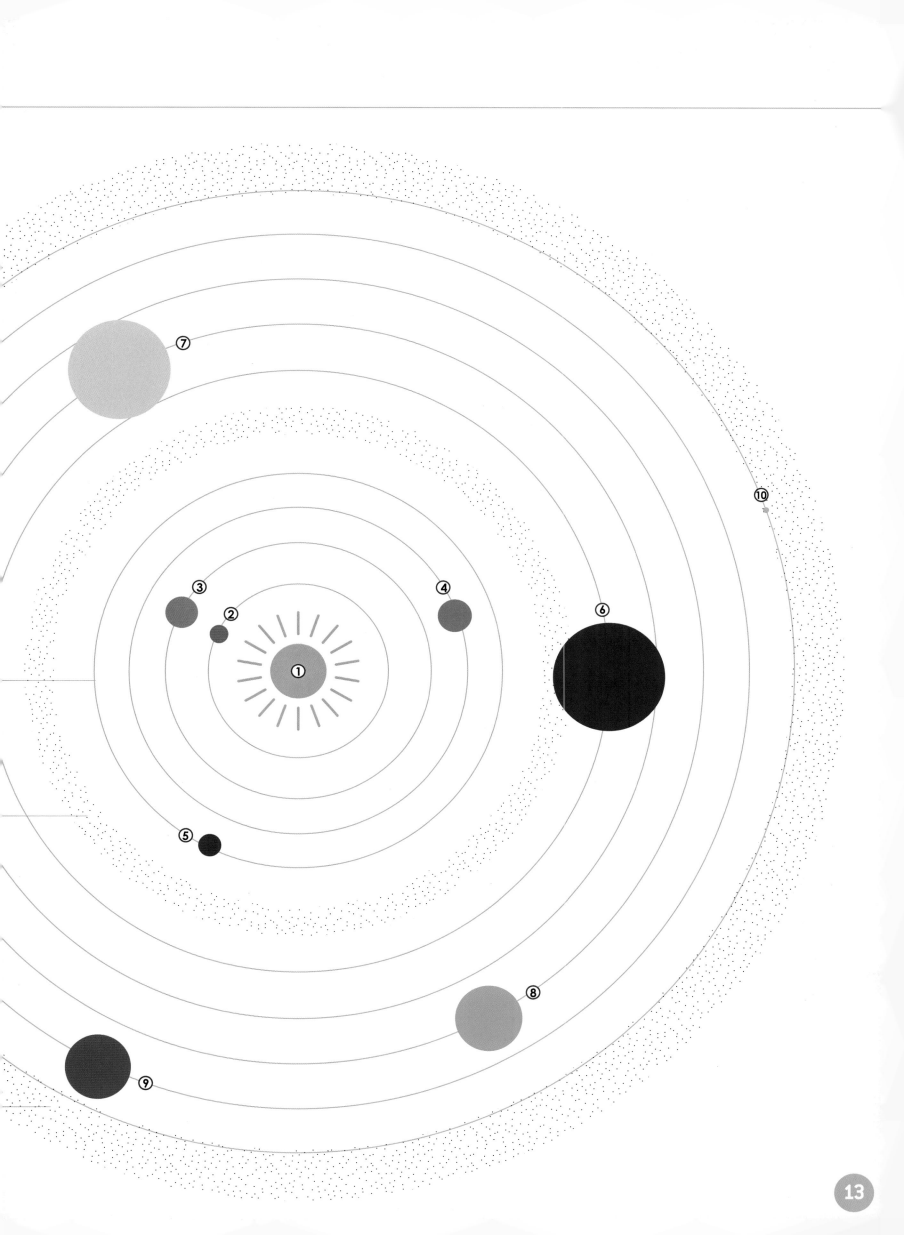

PLANETS OVERVIEW

The planets in our Solar System can be classified according to their structure, composition, size and features. A common classification divides the planets into three main groups. ⟶

TERRESTRIAL PLANET

A terrestrial planet or rocky planet, is a planet that is primarily composed of silicate rocks or metals. Within the Solar System, the terrestrial planets are the inner planets closest to the Sun.

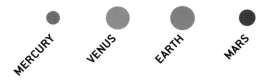

MERCURY   VENUS   EARTH   MARS

DAYS AND YEARS ON DIFFERENT PLANETS

Each planet has its peculiar orbit which differ one from another. The planets complete their revolution around the Sun at different times and speeds, which results in a different durations of years. Similarly, the time that planets takes to rotate around their axis varies from one another, giving different durations of days.

PERIOD OF ROTATION

The time a planet takes to rotate around its axis. Earth complete one rotation in 24 hours, or one day.

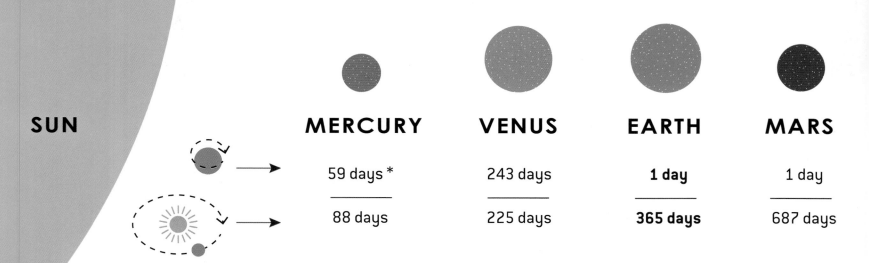

SUN	MERCURY	VENUS	EARTH	MARS
	59 days *	243 days	**1 day**	1 day
	88 days	225 days	**365 days**	687 days

*all time units refers to Earth's time measurement

GAS GIANT

A gas giant is a giant planet composed mainly of hydrogen and helium. Jupiter and Saturn are the gas giants of the Solar System.

JUPITER   SATURN

ICE GIANT

An ice giant is a giant planet composed mainly of heavy volatile substances, called ices. The ice giants of the Solar System are Uranus and Neptune.

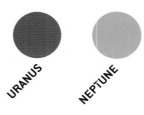

URANUS   NEPTUNE

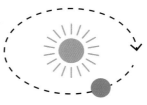

PERIOD OF REVOLUTION

The time a planet takes to orbit around the Sun. Earth makes it in 365 hours, what we call one 'solar year'.

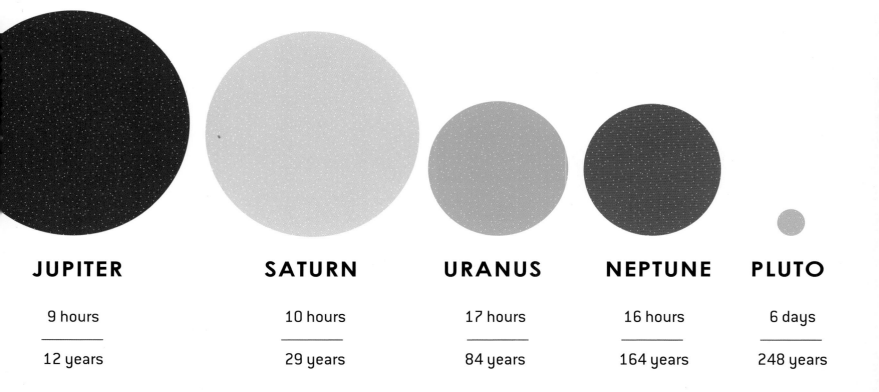

JUPITER	SATURN	URANUS	NEPTUNE	PLUTO
9 hours	10 hours	17 hours	16 hours	6 days
12 years	29 years	84 years	164 years	248 years

SATELLITES

Several spacecraft keep the Sun under constant observation, learning its secrets and warning Earth about dangerous space weather.

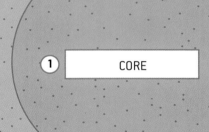

③ CONVECTIVE ZONE

② RADIATIVE ZONE

① CORE

SOLAR REGIONS

The Sun has six regions: the core, the radiative zone, and the convective zone in the interior; the visible surface, or photosphere, the chromosphere and the outermost region, the corona.

EXTREME TEMPERATURE

The temperature at the Sun's surface it's hot enough to make carbon, like diamonds and graphite, boil.

EARTH

1AU

93 million miles

ASTRONOMICAL UNITS

The astronomical unit, or AU, is defined by the distance from the Sun to Earth. This unit provides an easy way to quickly compare the distance of each planet from the Sun.

④ PHOTOSPHERE

⑤ CHROMOSPHERE

⑥ CORONA

SOLAR WIND

Electric currents in the Sun generate a magnetic field that is carried out through the Solar System by the solar wind — a stream of electrically charged gas blowing outward from the Sun in all directions.

THE SUN

Our Sun is a dwarf star. It is a ball of gas held together by its own gravity that doesn't have a solid surface.

The interaction between the Sun and the Earth makes our planet a suitable place for life. Though it is special to us, there are billions of stars like our Sun scattered across the universe.

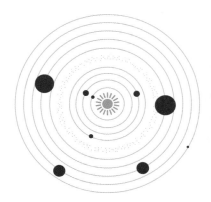

DIAMETER:

864,576 miles
109 times bigger than Earth

864,576 miles

TEMPERATURE

27,000,000 °F
core

9,932 °F
surface

COMPOSITION

92% Hydrogen, 7.8% Helium

DISCOVERY

In 1631 Thomas Harriott and Galileo Galilei observed Mercury with the newly invented telescope.

EXPLORING MERCURY

MESSENGER spacecraft was the first probe to orbit Mercury. It's main goal was understanding the smallest, densest and least-explored of the terrestrial planets.

MERCURY

Mercury is the planet closest to our
Sun and the smallest of the eight planets of the Solar System. Mercury is
hard to study because of its proximi-
ty to the Sun. Although slightly bigger
than Earth Moon, the planet is made
of heavy materials like iron, making it
much heavier than our satellite.

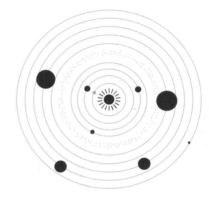

NAME ORIGIN:

Mercury was called after the messenger of the
Roman gods because he moves very quickly
around the Sun

DIAMETER:

3,032 miles
Mercury is 18 times smaller than Earth

TEMPERATURE:

-292 ºF on the side away from the Sun
806 ºF on the side facing the Sun

ATMOSPHERE:

Mercury has no atmosphere around to protect
it from the Sun or to retain heat

PLANET TYPE:

Terrestrial

MOONS:

Mercury has no moons

RINGS:

Mercury has no rings

TIME ON VENUS

A day on Venus lasts longer than a day on any other planet in our Solar System. The planet completes one rotation in 243 Earth's days.

INVERSE SPIN

Venus is one of just two planets of the Solar System that rotate from east to west. Only Venus and Uranus have this backwards rotation.

COLORS ON VENUS

From space, Venus is bright white because it is covered with clouds that reflect and scatter sunlight. The thick atmosphere filters the Sunlight so that everything would look orange if you were standing on Venus.

VENUS

Venus is the second planet from the Sun and our closest planetary neighbor. Similar in structure and size to Earth, Venus spins slowly in the opposite direction most planets do. Its thick atmosphere traps heat in a runaway greenhouse effect, making it the hottest planet in the Solar System.

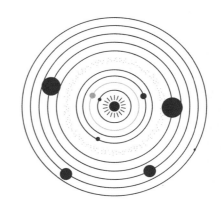

NAME ORIGIN:

Venus is named for the ancient Roman goddess of love and beauty

DIAMETER:

7,518 miles
Venus is almost as big as Earth

TEMPERATURE:

863 °F at surface

ATMOSPHERE:

Carbon dioxide, with clouds of sulfuric acid droplet

PLANET TYPE:

Terrestrial

MOONS:

Venus has no moons

RINGS:

Venus has no rings

SPACE MISSIONS

In 1975 the Soviet Union sent two spacecraft landers to Venus, Venera 9 and Venera 10. These were the very first landers to reach the planet's surface.

MAXWELL MONTES
36,089 ft

MOUNT EVEREST
29,029 ft

LANDSCAPE

Venus has mountains, valleys, and volcanoes. The highest mountain on Venus, Maxwell Montes, is 6,8 miles high, similar to the highest mountain on Earth, Mount Everest.

NAME ORIGINS

All of the other planets in the Solar System were named for Greek and Roman gods and goddesses. Differently, the name Earth is an English/ German word which simply refers to the ground.

A SINGLE MOON

Earth is the only planet that has only one moon. In many ways, our Moon is responsible for making Earth such a great home. For example, it stabilizes our planet's wobble, making the climate less variable.

EARTH

Earth is the third planet from the Sun and the fifth largest in the Solar System. Just slightly larger than nearby Venus, Earth is the biggest of the terrestrial planets. Our home planet is the only planet in our Solar System known to sustain life.

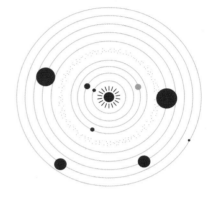

STRUCTURE

Earth is composed of four main layers. The inner and outer core are hot spheres made of iron and nickel. The mantle is a hot mixture of molten rock which has the consistency of caramel. Earth's crust includes the landscape we walk on and the bottom of the oceans.

SOLID CRUST
ROCKY MANTLE
OUTER CORE
INNER CORE

SHAPE

Earth is not a perfect sphere. In fact, it is an oblate spheroid - a sphere flattened at the poles. The diameter of the Earth at the equator is about 27 miles larger than the pole-to-pole diameter.

THE BLUE PLANET

Earth's oceans cover nearly 70 percent of the planet's surface and contains 97 percent of the water. Many of Earth's volcanoes are hidden under the ocean: some of them are taller than Mount Everest. Earth's longest mountain range is also found underwater, at the bottom of the Arctic and Atlantic oceans.

NAME ORIGIN:

Also known as the world, the name Earth is at least 1,000 years old and it simply means "ground"

DIAMETER:

7,926 miles

TEMPERATURE:

At surface: -126 °F min, 136 °F max
At core: 9,752 °F

ATMOSPHERE:

Nitrogen, Oxygen

PLANET TYPE:

Terrestrial

MOONS:

Earth has one moon

RINGS:

Earth has no rings

LUNA 2

The first spacecraft to make it to the Moon was the Luna 2. Made by the Soviet Union it reached the Moon in 1959 and the trip took 34 hours.

BAY OF DEW

SEA OF COLD

BAY OF RAINBOWS

SEA OF RAINS

LAKE OF DREAMS

SEA OF SERENITY

OCEAN OF STORMS

SEA OF VAPORS

SEA OF TRANQUILLITY

SEA OF FERTILITY

SEA OF CLOUDS

SEA OF MOISTURE

8.5 hours

HOW LONG TO GET THERE?

NASA undertook the shortest trip to the Moon in 2006. The probe New Horizons traveled at 36,000 miles per hour and arrived at the Moon in 8 and a half hours.

LUNAR SEAS

The lunar seas are large, dark, basaltic plains formed by ancient volcanic eruptions. They were dubbed "mária", Latin for "seas", by early astronomers who mistook them for actual seas.

EARTH'S MOON

Earth's Moon is the only place beyond Earth where humans have set foot. The brightest and largest object in our night sky, the Moon makes Earth a more livable planet by moderating our home planet's wobble on its axis, leading to a relatively stable climate. It also causes tides, creating a rhythm that has guided humans for thousands of years.

DIAMETER:

2,159 miles,
less than a third the width of Earth

DISTANCE FROM EARTH:

238,855 miles
the Moon is farther away from Earth than it seems:
30 Earth-sized planets could fit in between Earth and the Moon.

TEMPERATURE:

Min: -387 °F
Max: 253 °F

LUNAR LANDSCAPE

A steady rain of asteroids, meteoroids and comets strikes the surface of the Moon, leaving numerous craters behind. Tycho Crater is more than 53 miles wide.
Astronauts have left behind many debris on the Moon surface: these include six American flags and a camera.
The gravity on the surface of the Moon is one-sixth of Earth's, which is why in footage of moonwalks, astronauts appear to almost bounce across the surface.

FIRST MEN ON THE MOON

Apollo 11 was the first spacecraft to reach the Moon with humans on board in 1969. The astronauts Neil Armstrong and Buzz Aldrin walked on the Moon for a few hours, conducted some experiments and collected Moon rocks before their safely came back to Earth.

LUNAR PHASES

The changing illumination is why, from our perspective, the Moon goes through phases. During a "full moon," the hemisphere of the Moon we can see from Earth is fully illuminated by the Sun.
A "new moon" occurs when the side of the Moon facing us is having its night.

new moon

waning crescent

last quarter

waning gibbous

full moon

waxing gibbous

first quarter

waxing crescent

The Moon is slowly moving away from Earth, getting about 1 inch farther away each year.

MISSIONS

NASA's rover Curiosity is examining Martian rocks and soil at Gale Craterin searching for information that will reveal more about the present and past habitability of Mars, as well as whether humans could survive on Mars.

PHOENIX MARS' LANDERS

In 2008, NASA's Phoenix Mars lander was the first mission to touch water ice in the Martian arctic and to observe snow falling from clouds.

PHOBOS

DEIMOS

MARS' MOONS

Mars has two potato-shaped small moons. They were named for the characters Phobos (panic/fear) and Deimos (terror/dread) who, in Greek mythology, accompanied their father Ares (Mars) into battle.

MARS

Mars is a cold desert world, half the diameter of Earth. Like our planet, Mars has seasons, polar ice caps, volcanoes, canyons and weather, but its atmosphere is too thin for liquid water to exist for long on the surface. The red planet, as it is often called, is the fourth planet from the Sun. His red tint is due to a mineral called iron oxide that is common on the planet's surface.

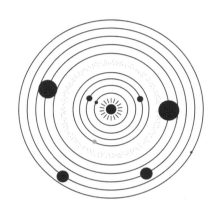

NAME ORIGIN:
Mars was named by the Romans for their god of war because of its red, bloodlike color

DIAMETER:
4,221 miles, half the diameter of Earth

TEMPERATURE:
At surface: -243 °F to 68 °F

ATMOSPHERE:
Carbon dioxide, nitrogen, argon

PLANET TYPE:
Terrestrial planet

MOONS:
Mars has 2 small moons

RINGS:
Mars has no rings

MARTIAN POLAR ICE CAPS
Mars has both North and South polar ice caps, as Earth does. Both ice caps are made mostly of frozen water. With so much water frozen in the ice caps of Mars, some scientists think that life could have once existed there.

OLYMPUS MONS

OLYMPUS MONS
The largest volcano in the Solar System, Olympus Mons, belongs to Mars. Olympus is also the highest mountain in the Solar System at more than 15 miles high, three times higher than Mount Everest.

MOUNT EVEREST

THE ASTEROID BELT

The Asteroid belt lies in the region between Mars and Jupiter, dividing the inner terrestrial planets from the outer giant planets. First discovered in 1801, it is made of thousands of rocks and debris that orbit around the Sun.

Most scientists believe that asteroids are material left over from the formation of the Solar System that never merged into a planet.
Many of the bigger asteroids have been given names.

MARS

ASTEROID BELT

JUPITER

Ceres is the largest object in the Asteroid belt and a dwarf planet. It comprises 25 percent of the Asteroid belt's total mass and its diameter is approximately 587 miles (945 km), almost four times smaller than Earth's Moon size (2,159 miles/3475 Km).

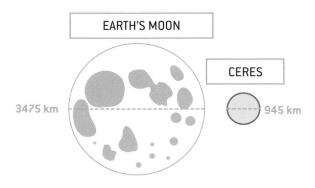

EARTH'S MOON

CERES

3475 km

945 km

PLUTO

KUIPER BELT

NEPTUNE

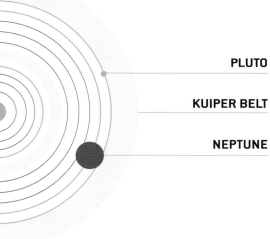

KUIPER BELTS

Similar to the Asteroid belt, the Kuiper belt is a disc-shaped region of icy bodies, including dwarf planets and comets which lies beyond the orbit of Neptune. It extends from about 30 to 55 AU and it's populated with hundreds of thousands of icy bodies larger than 60 miles.

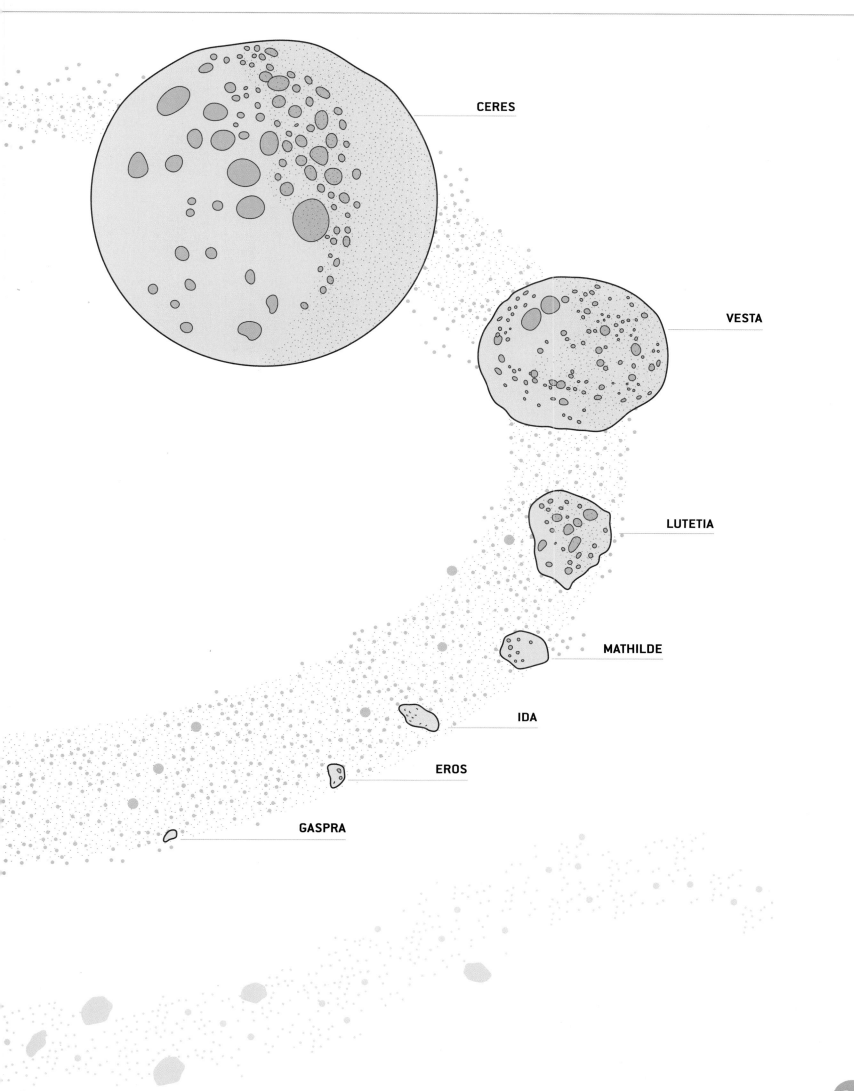

CERES

VESTA

LUTETIA

MATHILDE

IDA

EROS

GASPRA

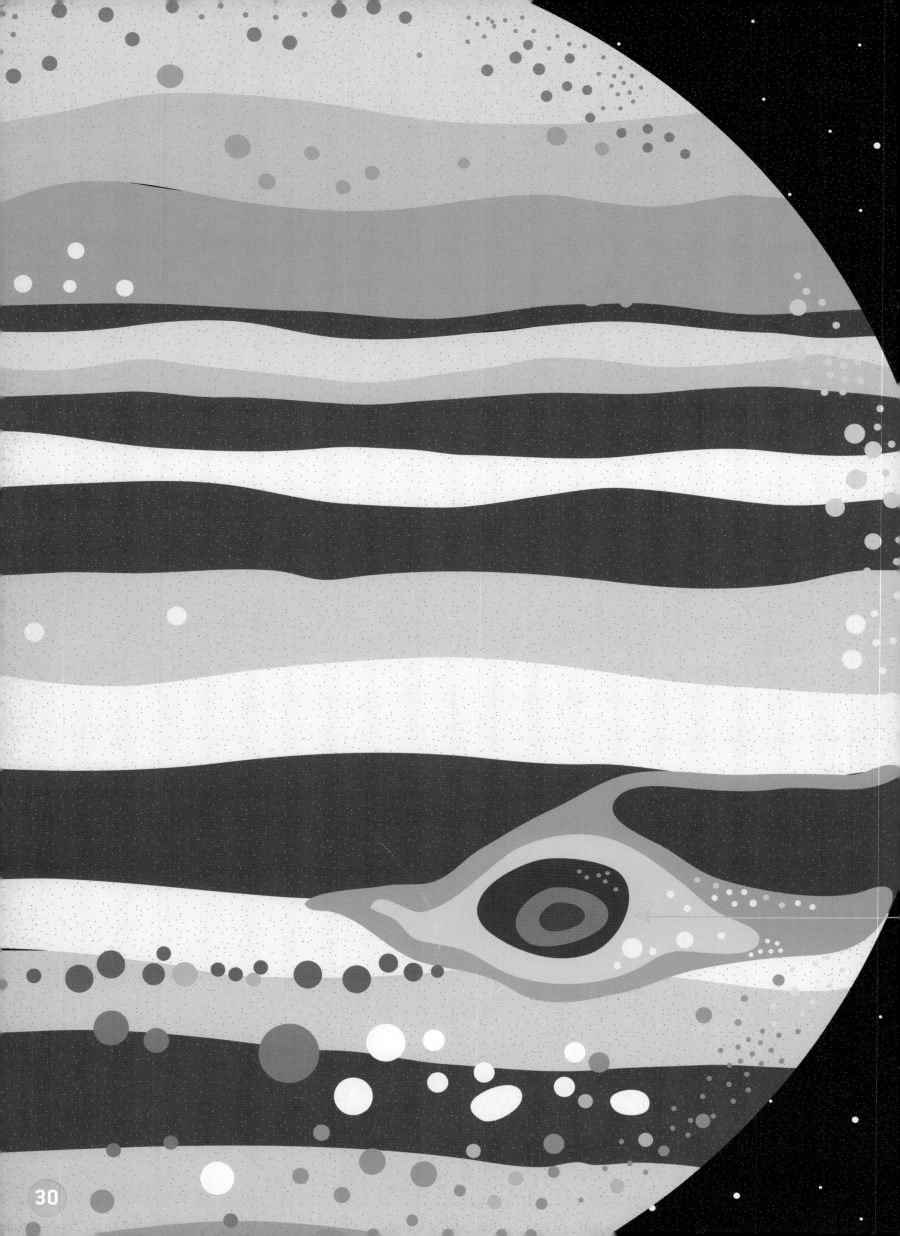

JUPITER

Jupiter is the largest planet in the Solar System and the first of the outer planets, crossed the Asteroid belt. Jupiter is so big that all the other planets in the Solar System could fit inside it. From Earth, it is the second brightest planet in the night sky, after Venus.

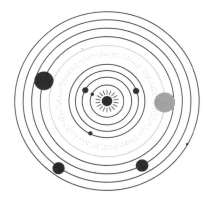

NAME ORIGIN:
Due to its majestic size, Jupiter is named for the king of ancient Roman gods

DIAMETER:
86,881 miles, 11 times wider than Earth

TEMPERATURE:
-229 °F, average

ATMOSPHERE:
Jupiter's atmosphere is made up mostly of hydrogen and helium

PLANET TYPE:
Gas-giant planet

MOONS:
Jupiter has 53 confirmed moons and 14 provisional moons, for a total of 67 satellites

RINGS:
Jupiter has three thin faint rings which are very hard to see

EXPLORATIONS
Many missions have visited Jupiter and its system of moons. Launched in 2011 and arrived to the planet on July 2016, the Juno spacecraft is currently orbiting Jupiter.

JUPITER'S MOONS
Scientists are most interested in the Galilean satellites – the four largest moons discovered by Galileo Galilei in 1610.

GANYMEDE

GALILEO

CALLISTO

IO

GREAT RED SPOT
Jupiter's Great Red Spot is a gigantic storm, about the size of Earth, that has been raging for hundreds of years.

EUROPA

SHORT DAYS
Jupiter spins faster than any other planet. While Earth takes 24 hours to rotate, a day on Jupiter lasts only 10 hours.

JUPITER'S MOONS

Jupiter is one of the most interesting planets in the Solar System. The gas giant itself is impressive; with cyclonic storms larger than the Earth and a magnetosphere so powerful it defies comprehension.

Jupiter has 53 named moons. 14 more have been discovered but not given official status or names. This means that Jupiter has 67 moons in total. Scientists are particularly interested in the first 4 moons discovered beyond Earth – the Galilean satellites.

VOLCANIC REALM

IO

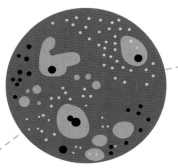

Io is the most volcanically active body in the Solar System. As Io travels in its slightly elliptical orbit, Jupiter's gravity causes "tides" in the solid surface that rise 330 ft high on Io, generating enough heat for volcanic activity and to drive off any water.

EUROPA

ROCKY CRUST

ROCKY MANTLE
IRON CORE

Europa, Callisto and Ganymede might all contain vast oceans of liquid water underneath icy shells. Therefore, the icy moons of Jupiter are probably the best place to look for life in the entire Solar System.

POTENTIAL FOR LIFE

Europa's surface is mostly made of water ice that may be covering an ocean of water beneath. The moon is thought to have twice as much water as Earth. With such abundance of liquid element, Europa intrigues astrobiologists because of its potential for other forms of life.

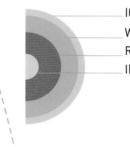

ICY CRUST
WATER OCEAN
ROCKY MANTLE
IRON CORE

THE OUTER MOON

Callisto's surface is heavily cratered and ancient, a visible record of events from the early history of the Solar System. Layer structure at Callisto is less well defined respect the other moons and it appears to be mainly a mixture of ice and rock.

ROCKY CRUST
ROCKY AND
ICY MANTLE
ROCKY CORE

GANYMEDE

THE BIGGEST MOON

Ganymede is the largest moon in the Solar System, larger than the planet Mercury and is the only moon known to have its own internally generated magnetic field.

ICY CRUST
WATER OCEAN
ICY MANTLE
ROCKY MANTLE
IRON CORE

TITAN

Saturn's largest satellite Titan is a bit bigger than planet Mercury. It is one of the few known moons to have a dense atmosphere, which might be very similar to what Earth's was like long time ago.

WINDY PLANET

It's pretty windy on Saturn. Winds around the planet's equator can reach 1,120 miles per hour. In comparison, the fastest winds on Earth reach only about 250 miles per hour.

SATURN

Adorned with thousands of beautiful rings and ringlets, Saturn is unique among the planets. All four gas giants have rings made of chunks of ice and rock, but none are as spectacular or as complicated as Saturn's. Like the other gas giants, Saturn is mostly a massive ball of hydrogen and helium.

SPACE MISSIONS

Orbiting Saturn and its numerous moons, the Cassini spacecraft is a keystone of exploration of the Saturnian system. Cassini was launched in 1997, reached Saturn in 2004 and is still studying the planet.

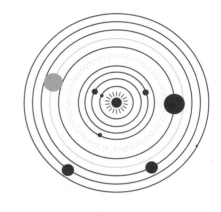

RINGS

Saturn's beautiful rings are visible from Earth even with a small telescope. They are not solid, but made up of particles of ice, dust and rock. Some are as tiny as grains of sand, some much larger than skyscrapers.

NAME ORIGIN:

Saturn is named for the Roman god of wealth and agriculture

DIAMETER:

74,900 miles
19.5 times bigger than the diameter of the Earth

TEMPERATURE:

The temperature at Saturn's upper atmosphere average around -283 ºF

ATMOSPHERE:

Saturn's atmosphere is made of hydrogen and helium

PLANET TYPE:

Gas-giant planet

MOONS:

Saturn has 53 confirmed moons and 9 provisional moons

RINGS:

Saturn has 7 rings

MOONS

While most of the satellites orbiting other planets take their names from Greek or Roman mythology, Uranus' moons are unique in being named for characters from the works of William Shakespeare and Alexander Pope.

OBERON

TITANIA

UMBRIEL

ARIEL

MIRANDA

PUCK

COMPRESSED HYDROGEN AND HELIUM

COMPRESSED WATER AND AMMONIA

ROCKY CORE

ICE PLANET

Uranus is one of the two ice giants in the outer Solar System. Most of the planet is made up of a dense fluid of icy materials — water, methane and ammonia — above a small rocky core.

URANUS

The seventh planet from the Sun with the third largest diameter in the Solar System, Uranus is cold and windy. It was discovered with the aid of a telescope in 1781 by astronomer William Herschel, who originally thought it was either a comet or a star.

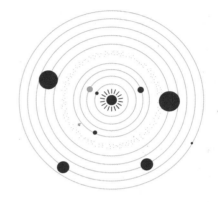

EXPLORATIONS

Only one spacecraft has visited distant Uranus. After traveling for nine years, NASA's Voyager 2 gathered critical information about the mysterious planet in just six hours.

A UNIQUE ROTATION

Like Venus, Uranus rotate from east to west. Unlike any of the other planets, Uranus rotates on its side, which means it spins horizontally.

RINGS

Uranus has two sets of rings. The inner system of nine rings consists mostly of narrow, dark gray rings. The two outer sets of rings are, respectively, reddish and blue in color.

NAME ORIGIN:

Uranus was named for the Greek god of the sky

DIAMETER:

31,763 miles, 4 times larger than Earth

TEMPERATURE:

-371 °F at surface,
9,000 °F at core

ATMOSPHERE:

Hydrogen, Helium, Methane

PLANET TYPE:

Ice giant

MOONS:

Uranus has 27 small moons and 9 provisional moons

RINGS:

Uranus has 13 faint rings

A SPECIAL BLUE

As for Uranus, Neptune's blue color is the result of methane in the atmosphere. Compared Uranus, Neptune is a more vivid, brighter blue, so there must be an unknown component that causes the color.

NEPTUNE

Neptune is the last of the hydrogen and helium gas giants in our Solar System. It's dark, cold and whipped by supersonic winds. More than 30 times as far from the Sun as Earth, Neptune takes almost 165 Earth years to orbit our star. In 2011 Neptune completed its first orbit since its discovery in 1846.

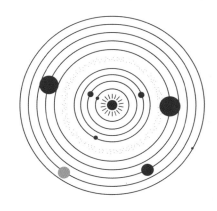

NAME ORIGIN:
Neptune was named for the Roman god of the sea

DIAMETER:
30,778 miles

TEMPERATURE:
-353 °F

ATMOSPHERE:
Hydrogen, Helium, Methane

PLANET TYPE:
Ice giant

MOONS:
Neptune has 14 known moons

RINGS:
Neptune has 6 known rings

DISCOVERY

Using the predictions of the astronomer Le Verrier, Johann Galle discovered Neptune in 1846. He wanted to name the planet for Le Verrier, but that wasn't accepted by the astronomical community. The planet was eventually named for Neptune, the god of the sea.

LE VERRIER

UNSUAL RINGS

Neptune has six known rings. These rings are not uniform but are made up of clumps of dust called arcs. The rings are thought to be relatively young and short-lived.

TRITON

Triton is the largest of Neptune's moons and the coldest objects in our Solar System. It is so cold that most of the nitrogen is condensed as frost. It's shiny surface reflects 70 percent of the Sunlight.

CHARON

Pluto has a very large moon, named Charon, that is almost half its size. Discovered in 1978, this moon is so large that Pluto and Charon are sometimes referred to as a double dwarf planet system.

HYDRA

NIX

OTHER MOONS

Pluto has four other, much smaller, moons. They are named Nix, Hydra, Kerberos, and Styx. They were discovered respectively in 2005, 2005, 2011, and 2012.

KERBEROS

STYX

EXPLORATIONS

NASA's New Horizons was the first mission to explore the Kuiper belt, home of most dwarf planets. The probe visited Pluto in July 2015: it took nine years to reach the planet from Earth.

PLUTO

Discovered in 1930 by the American astronomer Clyde Tombaugh, Pluto is a dwarf planet and a member of a group of objects that orbit in a disc-like zone beyond the orbit of Neptune called the Kuiper belt or trans-Neptunian objects.

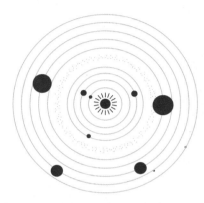

A RECLASSIFIED PLANET

Pluto was considered our Solar System's ninth planet until 2006. After the discovery of similar worlds, scientists decided to review the definition of planet. Because of its size and the weakness of its gravitational field, Pluto was reclassified as a dwarf planet.

TINY PLUTO

Pluto is about two-thirds the diameter of Earth's Moon and has probably a rocky core surrounded by a mantle of water ice. Pluto's gravity is extremely low, about six percent of Earth's.

EARTH'S MOON

PLUTO

EARTH

NAME ORIGIN:

Pluto derives its name from the Roman god of the underworld

DIAMETER:

1,475 miles, about 2/3 the diameter of Earth's Moon

TEMPERATURE:

-391 °F at surface

ATMOSPHERE:

Pluto's atmosphere is made of nitrogen, methane and carbon monoxide

PLANET TYPE:

Dwarf planet

MOONS:

Pluto has 5 moons

RINGS:

Pluto has no rings

MOONS AND RINGS

NAMED MOONS　　**UNNAMED MOONS**　　**RINGS**

MERCURY

VENUS

JUPITER

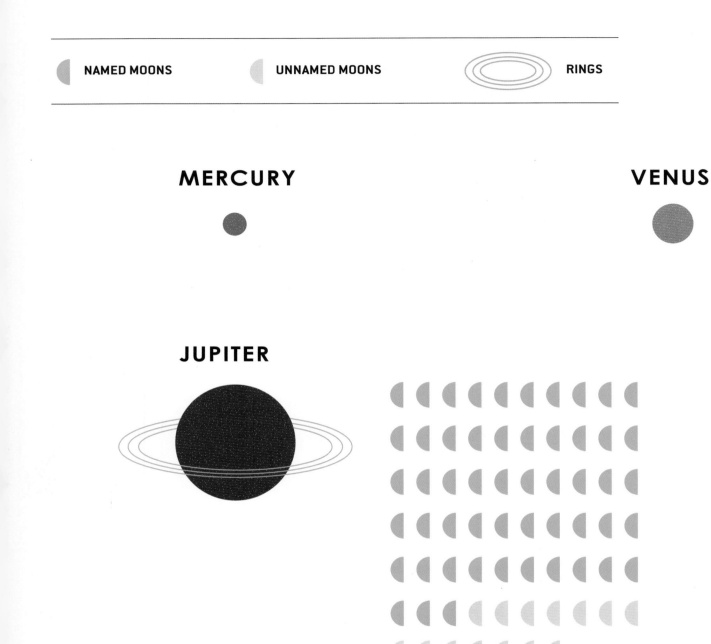

67 moons, 3 rings

URANUS

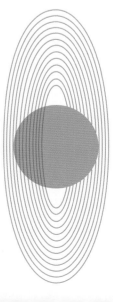

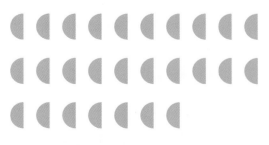

27 moons, 13 rings

EARTH

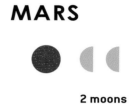

1 moon

MARS

2 moons

SATURN

62 moons, 7 rings

NEPTUNE

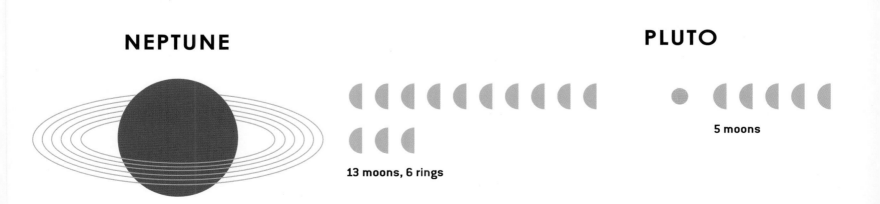

13 moons, 6 rings

PLUTO

5 moons

HOW LONG TO GET THERE?

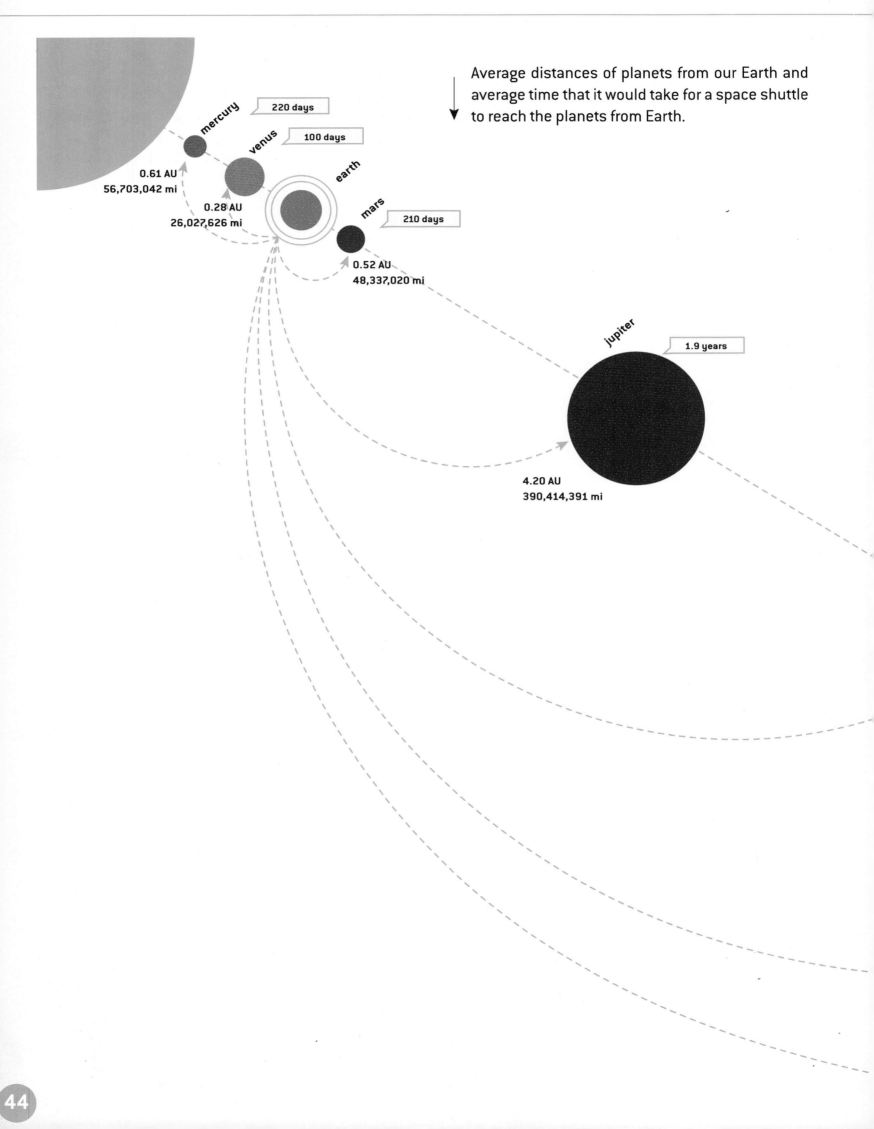

mercury · 220 days
0.61 AU
56,703,042 mi

venus · 100 days
0.28 AU
26,027,626 mi

earth

mars · 210 days
0.52 AU
48,337,020 mi

jupiter · 1.9 years
4.20 AU
390,414,391 mi

Average distances of planets from our Earth and average time that it would take for a space shuttle to reach the planets from Earth.

Imagine there was a space shuttle capable of traveling to every planet of the Solar System. How long would it take to reach each planet from Earth? It would depends on many factors such as the speed at lunch and the trajectory taken. The time to destination would also depends whether the space ship would just want to make a flyby or enter the orbit of another planet. In the second case, the time would double or even triple. In this page we assume to take the simplest approach and use the medium distance between Earth and the planets.

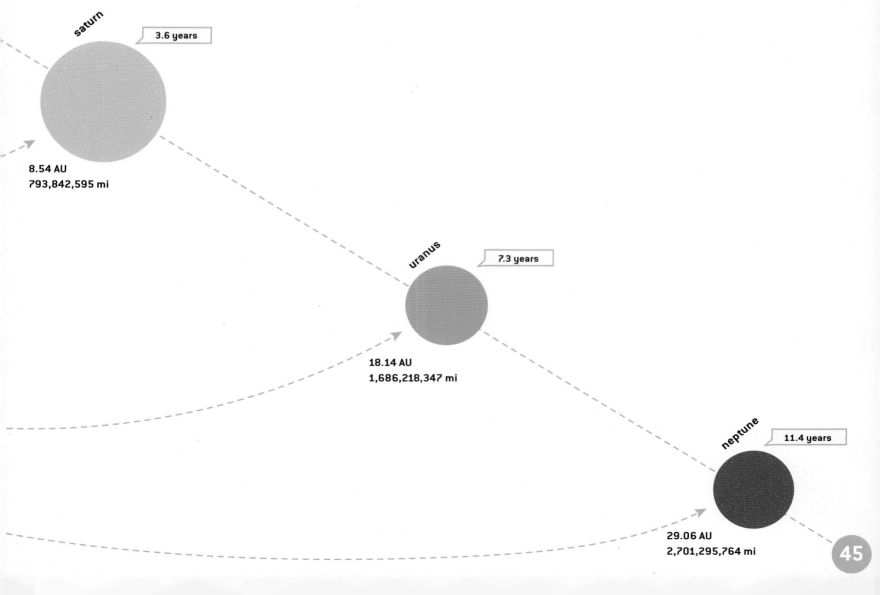

saturn

3.6 years

8.54 AU
793,842,595 mi

uranus

7.3 years

18.14 AU
1,686,218,347 mi

neptune

11.4 years

29.06 AU
2,701,295,764 mi

OUR GALAXY, THE MILKY WAY

The Solar System may seem big to us, but it is only a tiny part of a huge galaxy – the Milky Way. Our Sun is in fact one of at least 100 billion stars in the Milky Way, a spiral galaxy about 100,000 light years across. The stars are arranged in a pinwheel pattern with four main arms and we live about two-thirds of the way up one of them.

Like other spiral galaxies, the Milky Way has a bulge, a disk, and a halo which contain different objects. The halo and central bulge contain old stars and the disk is filled with gas, dust, and young stars. Our Sun is itself a fairly young star, only five billion years old. The Milky Way galaxy is at least five billion years older.

HOW MANY STARS?

Even though we can't actually count the stars in a galaxy, we can estimate the number of stars at roughly 100,000,000,000.

MAPPING A GALAXY

Mapping the Milky Way from planet Earth is very difficult. Clouds of dust permeate our galaxy, blocking the view of the stars. Today, astronomers have a suitable map of our galaxy's spiral structure, but like early explorers charting new territory, they continue to patiently fill in the blanks.

PERSEUS ARM

OUTER ARM

OUR SUN

A MYTHOLOGICAL GALAXY

In Greek mythology the Milky Way originates from the milk spilled from Hera's breast while refusing to feed baby Heracles. From Earth, the galaxy resemble a band of milky, shiny light lying over a black background.

WHERE THE STARS BORN

The arms of our galaxy are stuffed with gas and dust, the ingredients of stars. This is where most stars in the galaxy are born.

CENTRAL BLACK
HOLE

SCUTUM-CENTAURUS
ARM

SAGITTARIUS ARM

CENTRAL BLACK HOLE

All of the stars in the Milky Way orbit a super-massive black hole at the galaxy's center, which is estimated to be four million times as massive as our Sun.

SPACE SUMMARY

Although our galaxy contains a stunning number of stars, it is just a tiny part of the universe.
The Milky Way belongs to the Local Group, a neighborhood consisting of more than 54 galaxies that are gravitationally bound to each other.

Aside from our galaxy, the most massive one in this group is Andromeda, which appears to be on course to collide with the Milky Way in about four billion years from now.

HOW MANY SHAPES?

Scientists calculate that there are at least 100 billion galaxies in the observable universe, each one brimming with stars. Galaxies come in different sizes and shapes.

SPIRAL GALAXY

Disk shaped galaxies with a round, central hub. They rotate with spiral arms that contain interstellar dust and gas.

ELLIPTICAL GALAXY

The most common type of galaxy, they are minimal star formation with little structure where long lived stars abound.

SPHEROIDAL GALAXY

Low luminosity galaxies, similar to dwarf elliptical galaxies in appearance but approximately spheroidal in shape.

IRREGULAR GALAXY

Probably the result of a collision of galaxies, they contain a complex mix of interstellar gas and dust, old and young stars.

MILKY WAY

Our Galaxy is the second biggest galaxy in the Local Group.

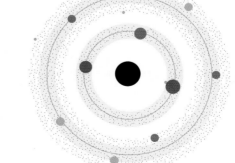

DRACO DWARF

The Draco Dwarf is a spheroidal galaxy and a satellite galaxy of the Milky Way.

ANDROMEDA

The Andromeda Galaxy is a spiral galaxy and the nearest major galaxy to the Milky Way. Its name comes from the area of the sky in which the constellation of Andromeda is located. The galaxy contains at least one trillion stars, twice the number of stars in the Milky Way. It is the biggest galaxy in the Local Group.

MESSIER 32

Messier 32 is a dwarf elliptical galaxy and a satellite galaxy of the Andromeda Galaxy.

TRIANGULUM GALAXY

The Triangulum Galaxy is a spiral galaxy located in the constellation of Triangulum. It is the third-largest member of the Local Group.

OTHER SUNS

A sun is a star, a ball of hydrogen and helium with enough mass that it can sustain nuclear fusion at its core. Our Sun is very big compared to the size of Earth, but is extremely small respect other suns that populate the universe. Stars come in many sizes, colors and varieties: a red star is cooler than a white star, and a white star is cooler than a blue star.

RED GIANT STARS

Aging stars become red giants and can be one hundred times larger than they were in their young phase. The red giant phase of a star's life will last a few hundred million years before it runs out of hydrogen and becomes a white dwarf.

WHITE DWARF STARS

When a star has completely run out of hydrogen fuel in its core, it becomes a white dwarf star. A white star still shines, but there's no fusion reactions happening any more.

Our Sun is a yellow dwarf star, possibly 4.6 billion years old

SUN   SIRIUS   POLLUX   ARCTURUS   RIGEL   ALDEBARAN

SUPER GIANT STARS

The largest stars in the universe are called supergiant stars. These are giants with dozens of times the mass of the Sun. Supergiant stars live fast and die young.

BETELGEUSE

ANTARES

GRAVITY

A black hole can not be seen because of the strong gravity that is pulling all of the light into its center. However, scientists can study the holes through the effects of its gravity on the stars and gases around it.

CENTER OF GALAXIES

Scientists think that every large galaxy has a supermassive black hole at its center.
The supermassive black hole at the center of the Milky Way galaxy is called Sagittarius A and has a mass equal to four million suns.

BLACK HOLES

A black hole is a place in space where gravity pulls so much that even light can not get out. The gravity is so strong because matter has been squeezed into a tiny space. This can happen when a star is dying.

Because no light can get out, black holes cannot be seen: they are invisible. Special space telescopes can help find black holes seeing how stars that are very close to black holes act differently than other stars.

TYPE OF BLACK HOLES

Black holes can come in a range of sizes, but three main types have been identified according to their mass and size.

MINIATURE BLACK HOLES

Formed during the Big Bang

STELLAR BLACK HOLES

Created from a dying, massive star

SUPERMASSIVE BLACK HOLES

Probably created from mass aggregation

SLOW ORBITS

Comets orbit the Sun like planets but it can take hundreds or even millions of years to complete one orbit around the Sun.

STAR SHOWERS

A few comets get close enough to be seen from Earth. When Earth passes through the tail of a comet, we see a meteor shower.

WHERE COMETS COME FROM

Most of the comets come from the dusty icy area around Pluto called the Kuiper belt.

COMETS

Comets are cosmic snowballs of frozen gases, rock and dust roughly the size of a small town. When a comet's orbit brings it close to the Sun, it heats up and spews dust and gases into a giant glowing head larger than most planets. The dust and gases form a tail that stretches away from the Sun for millions of miles.

Comets get their name from the Greek word "kometes" which means long hair, a reference to their long, shiny and fascinating tails.

HALLEY'S COMET

Halley's Comet is the most well known comet in the Solar System. As a periodic or short-term comet, it has orbital period that is less than 200 years, and has therefore been observed more than once by people over the centuries.

It's appearance in the skies above Earth has been noted since ancient times, and was associated with both bad and good omens by many cultures. Having been tracked for centuries, its visits have become entirely predictable.

SPACE ROCKS

Vesta is the largest known asteroid with a diameter of 329 miles. Asteroids come in different sizes: some bodies are smaller than 30 feet across.

VESTA

NAMING ASTEROIDS

Asteroids are named for a variety of different things, from real or fictional places (Atlantis, Utopia) to gods and celebrities. There are giant space rocks named for Star Trek's Mr. Spock, singer Stevie Wonder, actress Marilyn Monroe and philosophers such as Plato and Kant.

GALILEO

ASTEROIDS' MOONS

More than 150 asteroids are known to have a small companion satellite and in some cases even two small moons.

ASTEROIDS

Asteroids, sometimes referred to as minor planets, are rocky remnants left over from the early formation of the Solar System. Most of the asteroids in space can be found orbiting the Sun between Mars and Jupiter, within the Asteroid belt.

TYPE OF ASTEROIDS

Besides the asteroids that can be found within the Asteroid belt, astronomers have classified other asteroids, according to their behavior and provenience.

TROJANS

These asteroids share an orbit with a larger planet, but do not collide with it. The Jupiter trojans form the most significant population of trojan asteroids.

NEAR-EARTH ASTEROIDS

These objects have orbits that pass close by Earth's orbit. Asteroids that actually cross Earth's orbital path are known as Earth-crossers.

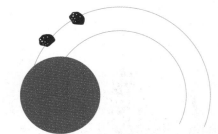

TUMBLING SPACE STONES

Most asteroids are irregularly shaped and they are often pitted or cratered. As asteroids revolve around the Sun in elliptical orbits, they also rotate, sometimes tumbling as they go.

MISSIONS

Several missions have flown by and observed asteroids. The Galileo spacecraft flew by asteroids Gaspra in 1991 and Ida in 1993. The Rosetta mission encountered asteroids Steins in 2008 and Lutetia in 2010.

ROSETTA

STEINS

LUTETIA

GIANT EXTINCTIONS

Early Earth experienced many large meteorite impacts that caused extensive destruction. A meteorite that impact 65 million years ago created a 190 miles wide crater on the Yucatan Peninsula and it's thought to have contributed to the extinction of the dinosaurs.

STARDUST

Scientists estimate that a stunning 48.5 tons of meteoritic material falls on the Earth each day.

METEORS & METEORITES

Little chunks of rock and debris in space are called meteoroids. They become meteors, or shooting stars, when they fall through a planet's atmosphere, leaving a bright trail as they are heated to incandescence by the friction of the atmosphere. Pieces that survive the journey and hit the ground are called meteorites.

TYPE OF METEORITES

There are three major types of meteorites: the irons, the stones, and the stony-irons. The majority of meteorites that fall to Earth are stony.

IRONS METEORITES

Originate from planetary cores

STONY METEORITES

Consist mostly of silicates

STONY-IRONS METEORITES

Consist of meteoric iron and silicates.

PERSEUS

METEOR SHOWERS

Around 30 meteor showers are visible from Earth every year. Meteor showers are named for the constellation where they seem to originate. The Perseids are named for the constellation of Perseus, one of the greatest Greek heroes. Perseids occur in August and were first recorded 2000 years ago.

Colorful DEBRIS

Meteors are sometimes observed with red, yellow or green trails. The colors are caused by the ionization of molecules while burning into the atmosphere.

WATER IN SPACE

Space explorations have demonstrated that the Solar System is rich in water. Scientists have discovered that some of the moons of the giant planets (Jupiter, Saturn, Uranus and Neptune) have hidden oceans locked inside a shell of ice. We know from Earth, itself an ocean world, that where there is water there is a potential for life. Could the alien, frozen oceans of the outer Solar System host unknown life forms? NASA is planning new space missions to try to answer the question.

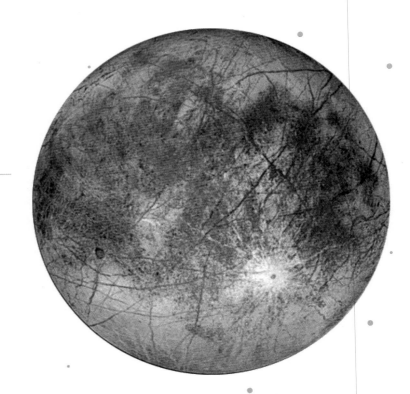

EUROPA

The smallest of Jupiter's Galilean moons. A salty ocean is believed to lie beneath Europa's icy crust.

Diameter: **1,939.6 miles**
Surface temperature: **-276 °F**

 **ORBITS JUPITER**

ENCELADUS

A global ocean deep beneath the surface of this Saturn moon feeds jets of material that spray from the moon's surface into space.

Diameter: **313.2 miles**
Surface temperature: **-324 °F**

ORBITS SATURN

TITAN

Saturn's largest moon could have a subsurface ocean possibly as salty as the Dead Sea on Earth.

Diameter: **3,199.6 miles**
Surface temperature: **-290 °F**

 **ORBITS SATURN**

TRITON

Diameter: **1,681.9 miles**
Surface temperature: **-391 °F**

 **ORBITS NEPTUNE**

THE INTERNATIONAL SPACE STATION

The International Space Station is a very large spacecraft which orbits about 205 miles above Earth. It is a home for astronauts during their missions and a science laboratory made and used in collaboration between many countries.

The space station is made of many pieces that were put together in space by astronauts. The first piece was launched in 1998 by a Russian rocket. The first crew to perform a long-duration stay arrived in 2000. The International Space Station will be completed in 2017: astronauts use it to learn about living and working in space.

A HOME FOR ASTRONAUTS

The space station is as big inside as a five bedrooms house. It has two bathrooms, a gymnasium and a big bay window. There are usually three to six crew members at all times, but there can be as many as eight.

The journey to the spacecraft takes only six hours per way and is taken on the Russian spacecraft Soyuz.

SOYUZ

LABORATORIES

There are sixteen countries involved in the International Space Station. The laboratories inside the station are divided into blocks, according to the nations that work in it.

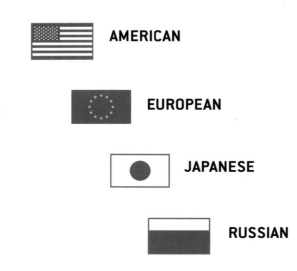

AMERICAN

EUROPEAN

JAPANESE

RUSSIAN

DAY AND NIGHT ON THE STATION

The International Space Station orbits the Earth once every 90 minutes, which means the Sun sets and rises for the crew 16 times a day.

SOLAR ARRAYS

Collect energy from the Sun and turn sunlight into electricity.

ROBOTIC ARMS

Helped to build the space station and can move astronauts around outside and control science experiments.

CUPOLA

A seven windows observatory where astronauts can enjoy the view of outer space and Earth below.

DOCKING PORTS

Doors that allow visiting spacecraft to connect to the space station.

HOW'S LIFE ON A SPACECRAFT?

Astronauts in space experience the absence of gravity, which means they can float in air without feeling their body weight. The sensation can be compared to diving into the ocean: hair stay straight in the air and there is no "up" or "down". To move around spacecraft, astronauts push themselves and gently fly from one part to another.

MORNING ROUTINE

Astronauts living and working in space have the same hygiene routine as people on Earth, but they have to follow some special rules. Astronauts wash their hair with a special rinseless shampoo, and go to the bathroom using specific procedures. After brushing their teeth, they usually swallow the toothpaste or spit it into paper.

SPACE EXPERIMENTS

Experiments carried on in space vary in nature: from growing vegetables to observing ant colonies and testing 3D printing in zero-gravity. Medical experiments are also carried on in space, mainly to study the effects of long-term missions on the human body.

SWEET DREAMS IN SPACE

Due to microgravity inside the spacecraft astronauts are weightless and can sleep in any orientation. They have to attach themselves so they don't float around and bump into something. Space station crews usually sleep in sleeping bags located in small individual cabins.

FREE SPACE TIME

Astronauts like to have fun, too. A popular pastime while orbiting Earth is simply looking out of the Cupola. Sunsets and sunrises are very spectacular, occurring every 45 minutes above Earth's atmosphere.
On any given day, crew members can watch movies, play music, read books, play cards and talk to their relatives on Earth.

DRINKING IN SPACE

Water spilled in space doesn't flow down, it merges into bubbles that can be sucked by astronauts to drink. To brush their teeth astronauts use a small bubble of water which sticks to their toothbrush.

HOW LONG UP THERE?

Missions on the International Space Station usually last about six months. But they can be very much longer: in 1994 Russian cosmonaut Valeriy Polyakov spent 437 days in space during a single mission.

**COSMONAUT
VALERIY POLYAKOV**

SPACE FOOD

There is a kitchen on the spacecraft where astronauts can prepare their meals. Some foods can be eaten in their natural forms, such as cookies and fruit, while other foods require adding water, such as noodles and scrambled eggs. Salt and pepper are available only in a liquid form. Astronauts can't sprinkle spices on their food in space as they would float away and go everywhere inside the spacecraft.

SPACE EXERCISE

Exercise is an important part of the daily routine for astronauts aboard the station to prevent bone and muscle loss. On average, astronauts exercise two hours per day. The equipment they use is different and needs to be specially designed for use in space.

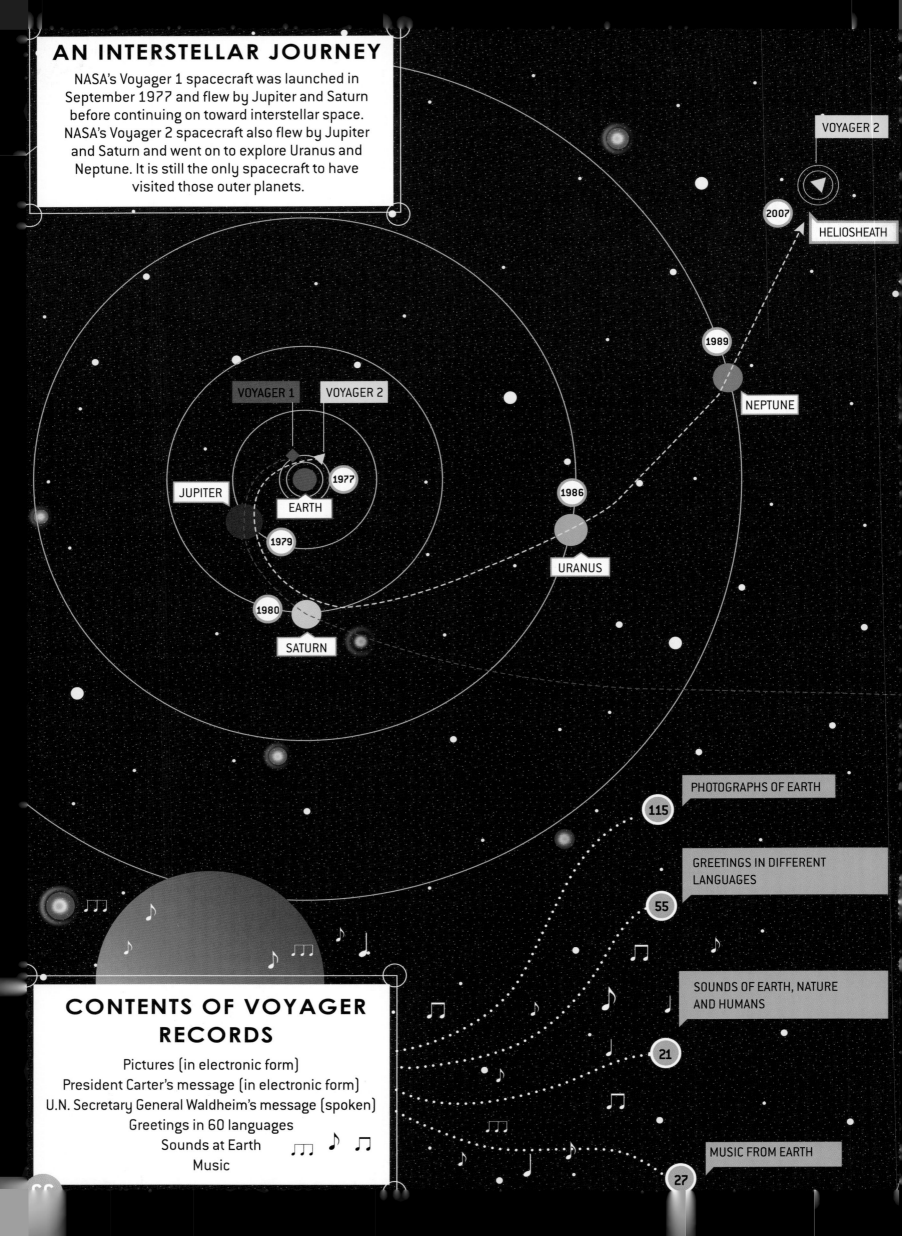

AN INTERSTELLAR JOURNEY

NASA's Voyager 1 spacecraft was launched in September 1977 and flew by Jupiter and Saturn before continuing on toward interstellar space. NASA's Voyager 2 spacecraft also flew by Jupiter and Saturn and went on to explore Uranus and Neptune. It is still the only spacecraft to have visited those outer planets.

VOYAGER 2

2007

HELIOSHEATH

1989

NEPTUNE

1986

URANUS

VOYAGER 1   VOYAGER 2

1977

JUPITER

EARTH

1979

1980

SATURN

PHOTOGRAPHS OF EARTH

115

GREETINGS IN DIFFERENT LANGUAGES

55

SOUNDS OF EARTH, NATURE AND HUMANS

21

CONTENTS OF VOYAGER RECORDS

Pictures (in electronic form)
President Carter's message (in electronic form)
U.N. Secretary General Waldheim's message (spoken)
Greetings in 60 languages
Sounds at Earth
Music

MUSIC FROM EARTH

27

VOYAGERS

The twin spacecraft Voyager 1 and 2 were launched in 1977. Part of the Voyager program was to fly by Jupiter and Saturn as well as to study the outer Solar System. At present, the Voyagers are the farthest spacecraft from Earth, exploring where no other object made by humans has been before. Continuing on their more than 39 years journey, the spacecraft still communicate with the Deep Space Network to receive routine commands and return data. In August 2012, Voyager 1 entered the interstellar space. Voyager 2 has crossed into the heliosheath, the outermost layer of the heliosphere, and is leaving the Solar System.

INTERSTELLAR SPACE

Scientists define the beginning of interstellar space as the place where the Sun's magnetic field stop affecting its surroundings. This place is called the heliopause and marks the end of a region created by our Sun and the beginning of an empty space between a star and another.

VOYAGER 1

INTERSTELLAR SPACE

2012

VOYAGER SPACECRAFT

A MESSAGE TO THE COSMOS

Spacecraft Voyager 1 and Voyager 2 carry aboard a very ambitious message which is intended to communicate a story of our world to any extraterrestrial form of life that might find them in the distant future. The Voyager message is carried by a phonograph record, a 12-inch gold-plated copper disk containing recordings of Earth's sounds, music and images selected to portray the diversity of life and culture on Earth, as well as a greeting message by the president of the United States James Earl Carter to the cosmos.

SPACE GLOSSARY

A

ASTEROID

Small rocky celestial body. Asteroids are found mostly in the region between the orbits of Mars and Jupiter. They are thought to be rocky fragments dating back to the formation of the Solar System that have never merged into a single planet.

ASTEROID BELT

The Asteroid belt is located between the orbits of Mars and Jupiter, and it separates the inner rocky planets from the outer gas and ice giants. It is made up of hundreds of thousands of rocks and debris that rotate captured in orbit by the Sun's gravity. The largest celestial body of the belt is Ceres, a dwarf planet, with a diameter equal to a quarter of that of the Moon.

ASTROBIOLOGY (EXOBIOLOGY)

It is a branch of biology that aims at searching and studying extra terrestrial life forms.

ASTRONAUT

Anyone traveling into space on board of a vehicle or a spaceship.

ATMOSPHERE

Gaseous envelope that surrounds a planet.

B

BLACK HOLE

It is an area in space where gravity is so strong that nothing inside it can escape, not even light. Typically they are formed after the "death" of a star, when it collapses on itself, concentrating a huge mass in a very confined space.

C

COMET

Similar to an asteroid, it is a relatively small celestial body consisting essentially of frozen gases, rock and dust. When a comet, following its orbit, gets close to the Sun, it begins to emit gas and dust and creates a long tail that can even be millions of miles long.

D

DWARF PLANET

It is a celestial body big enough to have a spherical shape, but not enough to occupy its orbit around the Sun by itself. Ceres, in the Asteroid belt, and Pluto in the Kuiper one, are two dwarf planets.

G

GALAXY

It is a large set of stars, of systems, gas and dust held together by the force of gravity. The galaxies are classified in accordance with size (ranging from dwarf galaxies, containing a few tens of millions of stars, to the giant galaxies, containing billions of stars) and form (they can be spiral, elliptical, spheroidal or irregular).

K

KUIPER BELT

Disk-shaped region of our Solar System, similar to the Asteroid belt (but 20 times larger), located beyond the orbit of Neptune at a distance of between 30 and 55 AU from the Sun. This includes small bodies composed by icy substances (such as water, ammonia and methane).
The belt includes comets, dwarf planets and hundreds of thousands of objects with a diameter exceeding 60 miles.

L

LANDER (VEHICLE OF LANDING, LANDING FORM)

Type of spacecraft designed to land softly on a celestial body.

LUNAR LANDING

The descent of a vehicle on the Moon. It can be a *soft landing*, when the descent of the vehicle is braked and controlled by rockets so that it lands intact, or a *hard landing* when the descent leads to the destruction of the vehicle, following its impact with the lunar soil.

M

METEOROID (METEORITE)

Fragment of loose rock in space. When a meteoroid enters the atmosphere of a planet, it becomes incandescent due to friction with the air, leaving a fiery trail: this is a meteor (also called "shooting star"). If a meteor lands on Earth it takes the name of meteorite. The mass of a meteorite is highly variable and ranges from a few ounces to several tons.

MOON

The only natural satellite of the Earth, it orbits at 238,855 miles around our planet. To Earth it always turns the same face, so that its hidden face was a mystery until the begin of the era of space exploration. We call "moon" any natural satellite that revolves around a planet.

O

ORBIT

It is the curved path that an object makes around a point in space due to gravity. For example: the Moon orbits around the Earth and the Earth, along with the other planets of the Solar System, revolves around the Sun in an elliptical orbit.

P

PERIOD OF REVOLUTION

The time it takes a planet (or any celestial body) to make a complete orbit around the Sun. The Earth takes 365 days (a calendar year) to make a complete revolution.

PERIOD OF ROTATION

The time it takes a planet (or any celestial body) to complete a rotation around its own axis. The Earth takes 24 hours (one day) to complete a rotation.

PLANET

Planets are spheroid celestial bodies that revolve around a star. Each planet follows its own orbit, that is not occupied by any other equally large or larger celestial body. Planets are mainly divided into: terrestrial (or rocky) planets, primarily composed of silicate rocks and metals; gas giants, mainly composed of hydrogen and helium; ice giants, formed by substances that are heavier than helium and hydrogen (water, ammonia and methane for example) that astrophysicists call "ice".

PROBE

Small space vehicle with no crew and equipped with sensors. The probe is loaded with the minimum fuel needed to accomplish its mission.

R

ROVER

A rover (that can also mean "tramp") is a wheeled vehicle designed to be carried on board of a lander on a planet or a satellite. It can be piloted by astronauts (as in the case of the lunar rover) and be designed to transport people and equipment, or it can be automated and controlled by a remote control (as in the case of the Mars rovers, Sojourner, Spirit, Opportunity and Curiosity).

S

SATELLITE

Any celestial body that revolves around a bigger celestial body (the Moon is the Earth's satellite). Even artificial vehicles that are launched from Earth in space orbit around our planet or another celestial body with a variety of purposes: from taking scientific measurements (for example meteorological

satellites), to facilitate communications and even to communicate or to detect movements and coordinates (satellites of Global Position System or military spy satellites).

STAR

Celestial body that emits light by its own. Stars are made of mostly hydrogen and helium, have large masses and produce energy through the fusion processes that take place in their nucleus. Stars are classified based on their color (that is correlated with their temperature) and their size. Our Sun, for example, is a yellow dwarf hotter than a red giant as Betelgeuse but colder than a white star like Sirius.

SUBORBITAL ALTITUDE

It's the altitude reached by any object launched into space that does not complete a full revolution around the Earth, or around the body from which it was launched.

V

V2

V2 were pilot-less vehicles designed for the Nazi army by the German engineer Wernher Von Braun in 1942. They were the first human-made objects to exit the atmosphere reaching an altitude of 62 miles. They were however also terrible weapons that killed hundreds of men, mainly in Great Britain.

GIULIA DE AMICIS

Born in Milan in 1986, after
completing her MSc in design she
started to work as an information
designer and illustrator for
small studios, newspapers and
environmental Ngos.
So far she has been studying
and living in Italy, Spain, India
and Greece.
She currently works and lives
in Brighton, UK.

VALENTINA FIGUS
Graphic layout

White Star Kids® is a registered trademark
property of White Star s.r.l.

© 2017 White Star s.r.l.
Piazzale Luigi Cadorna, 6
20123 Milan, Italy
www.whitestar.it

ISBN 978-88-544-1144-9
1 2 3 4 5 6   21 20 19 18 17

Printed in Poland